Everyday Science Experiments

Shadows in the Bedroom

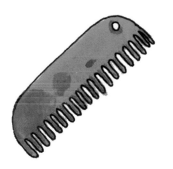

Susan Martineau
Illustrated by Leighton Noyes

with thanks to Kathryn Higgins,
Head of Chemistry, Leighton Park School

WINDMILL
BOOKS ™
New York

Published in 2012 by Windmill Books, An Imprint of Rosen Publishing
29 East 21st Street, New York, NY 10010

© 2012 b small publishing ltd
Adaptations to North American Edition © 2012 Windmill Books, An Imprint of Rosen Publishing

Library of Congress Cataloging-in-Publication Data

Martineau, Susan.
Shadows in the bedroom / by Susan Martineau. – 1st ed.
p. cm. – (Everyday science experiments)
Includes index.
ISBN 978-1-61533-372-1 (lib. bdg.) – ISBN 978-1-61533-410-0 (pbk.) –
ISBN 978-1-61533-472-8 (6-pack)
1. Science – Experiments – Juvenile literature. 1. Title.
Q164.M27538 2012
507.8 – dc22
                                    2010052124

Manufactured in the United States of America

CPSIA Compliance Information: Batch #BS2011WM: For Further Information contact Windmill Books, New York, New York at 1-866-478-0556

contents

How to Be a Scientist

Scientists do experiments to learn about the world. The experiments in this book will teach you about the science in your bedroom. You won't need any special equipment. These experiments use things you probably have at home already. Ask a grown-up before taking things for an experiment. Always make sure you have everything you will need before starting an experiment.

BE SAFE!
Never play with the electrical outlets and plugs in your bedroom.

5

Shadow Fun

This experiment is best done at night when it's really dark. Close the curtains and get ready to make some scary shapes. You can make funny shapes, too.

1. Cut a scary shape out of heavy paper.

2. Hold it in front of you, with a plain wall behind it.

3. Shine a flashlight or lamp on the shape.

Let's Take a Closer Look!

The holes you cut let the light from the flashlight or lamp through. The paper itself blocks the light, though. You get a shadow on the wall in the shape of your paper cutout. A shadow is made because the light cannot get through the paper.

Try This!

Try putting your hands together as shown to make the shape of a horse's head appear on the wall! Put your hands between the lamp and the wall.

See what happens when you move the shape close to or far from the lamp.

7

Clever Eyes

Light bounces off of everything we look at and into our eyes. This is how we see things. Our eyes need to let in just the right amount of light, though. Ask a friend to help you with this experiment.

1. Close the curtains.

2. Carefully point a flashlight upward so that some light shines on one side of your friend's face.

3. Look at the eye that the light is shining on and the eye in darkness. See what is different about them.

Cats can't see any better than we can in the daylight!

Let's Take a Closer Look!

The eye in the light has a smaller black part, or **pupil**, than the eye in the shadows. Light enters the eye through the pupil. The pupil gets smaller to stop too much light from hurting the inside of the eye. The pupil gets bigger to let in more light when we need to see in the dark.

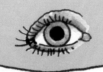

Quick Fact

The colored part of your eye is called the **iris**. It is the muscle that controls the size of the pupil.

Did You Know?

Cats hunt at night. The pupils of their eyes can open extra wide to let in as much light as possible. This helps them see well in the dark.

Mirror Magic

Have you ever wondered why you can see yourself in a mirror? Did you know you can use mirrors to look behind you, too? You will need a friend to help with this mirror magic.

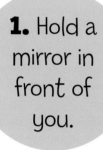

1. Hold a mirror in front of you.

2. Ask your friend to stand behind you.

3. Move the mirror until you see your friend in it!

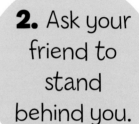

Let's Take a Closer Look!

You can see yourself in a mirror because light **rays** bounce off you and into the mirror. The mirror is very shiny and bounces the rays back so that you see a **reflection** of yourself. Light rays bounce off your friend, too, and are bounced back by the mirror. You then see the friend's reflection.

Quick Quiz!

What do car drivers use to see behind them?

Quick Warning!

Be careful when you are holding mirrors. They can break very easily.

Try This!

See what happens to reflections when you tape two small mirrors together. Put a small object in front of the mirrors. Move them closer together and farther apart. Count the reflections.

Hold one mirror in front of you and one behind you to see the back of your head!

Mad Mirrors

When you look in a mirror, you do not always see the reflection you might expect to see. This is very useful for tricks! Use a bit of sticky tack to keep the mirror steady.

1. Stand a small mirror upright.

2. Ask a friend to write his or her name on a piece of paper.

3. Put the paper in front of the mirror.

Let's Take a Closer Look!

Your friend's name appears reversed in the mirror! Reflections are always the wrong way around. If you wave at yourself with your right hand in a mirror, it will look as if you are waving your left hand. It is called a mirror image.

Try This!

Find a full-length mirror. Stand very close to the edge of it. Lift one arm and one leg.

If you don't have a full-length mirror at home, try this in a clothing store!

Electric Tricks

We use lots of electricity in our homes. It powers everything from lights to computers. This kind of electricity moves through wires inside our houses. There's also another sort of electricity that we can make ourselves!

1. Tear a tissue into small pieces.

2. Find a plastic comb.

3. Comb your clean, dry hair about 20 times.

4. Hold the comb close to the bits of tissue.

Let's Take a Closer Look!

When you run the comb through your hair over and over again, this makes **static electricity** build up in the comb. This static electricity pulls the tissue paper toward the comb and makes it jump like magic.

Turn the lights off when you leave your bedroom.

Don't waste electricity!

Quick Warning!

Never play with the electrical outlets or wires in your house.

Did You Know?

Static electricity builds up in clouds during thunderstorms. It gets so powerful that it jumps to other clouds or to the ground in the form of a huge spark, or lightning.

Sticking Together

Gather all sorts of things from around your bedroom, such as stuffed animals, coins, pencils, plastic and metal buttons, pencils, pencil sharpeners, books, and keys. You'll also need a magnet.

1. Spread your collection of things on the floor.

2. Touch each one with the magnet.

3. Note what happens to each object.

If you don't have horseshoe magnet ~~like~~ e the one on page 16, use one from your refrigerator.

Let's Take a Closer Look!

The magnet does not stick to everything. Magnets have a special, invisible power that pulls iron and steel things toward them. Most metal objects stick to a magnet. Things made of paper, wood, or fabric don't, though.

Quick Quiz!

Will your magnet pick up a pencil?

Try This!

If you have a few magnets, test them to see which is the strongest. Make a pile of paper clips and see which magnet can pick up the most.

Quick Warning!

Never put magnets near computers, telephones, or watches. Magnets can damage these things.

Waves of Sound

Sounds are invisible waves traveling through the air. They are all around us. For this experiment, you will need to make a cone out of a piece of paper.

1. Secure the cone with tape. Trim the wide end.

2. Tape the cone around one end of some thin plastic tubing.

3. Hold the cone's wide end over a ticking clock or watch.

4. Put the free end of the tube just inside your ear.

Let's Take a Closer Look!

The cone collects the sounds of the clock and sends them down the tube to reach your ear. They sound louder because they are being squeezed down a narrow tube. Sound waves normally spread out. However, the tube is like a narrow path leading them to your ear.

Quick Quiz!

What's the name of the gadget doctors use to listen to your heart?

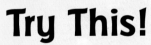

Try This!

Hold the cone over your radio or the speaker of your music player. Put the other end of the tube in your ear. Who needs headphones?

Don't push the tube too hard into your ear!

Pulse Power

Your heart pumps blood all around your body. It works harder when you are running around and slows down again when you are sitting still or lying in bed. In this experiment, you will see how fast your blood is pumping around.

1. Hold one hand out with the palm up.

2. Look at where the hand joins the wrist, below the thumb.

3. Place the first two fingers of the other hand here.

4. Press down lightly with those fingers.

Let's Take a Closer Look!

You should be able to feel a flickering movement under the skin. This is your **pulse**. Each time your heart beats, it is sending blood around your body to give you energy. Each pulse movement you feel is a heartbeat.

Quick Fact

You can also find a pulse in your neck, your temple, your elbow, and even the back of your knee.

Try This!

Jump up and down or bounce on your bed for two minutes. Time yourself with a bedside clock or your watch. Feel how fast your pulse is going now. Check your pulse again after lying still in bed for five minutes.

If you are fit and healthy, it doesn't take long for your pulse to slow down again!

Measure Yourself!

How tall are you? How heavy are you? How big are your feet? Try keeping a growth chart for a year to see how you change. Instead of your shoe size, you could also write in how long your feet are in inches (cm).

MONTH	HEIGHT	WEIGHT	SHOE SIZE

1. Draw a chart on a large piece of paper, as shown.

2. Ask a friend to measure how tall you are each month.

3. Weigh yourself and write in your shoe size, too.

4. Keep the chart on your wall or pinned inside your closet door.

Did You Know?

The tallest person ever recorded was Robert Wadlow. By the age of eight, he was tall enough to carry his dad up the stairs! He grew to be 8 feet 11 inches (2.72 m) tall.

When you weigh yourself, take off your shoes and coat!

Quick Fact

People stop growing between the ages of 16 and 19.

Let's Take a Closer Look!

When you are young, your body is growing all the time. Ask your friends to keep growth charts of their weights, heights, and shoe sizes, too. You will see that some people grow more quickly or more slowly than others.

READ MORE

Jackson, Tom. *Experiments with Light and Color.* Cool Science. New York: Gareth Stevens, 2010.

Robinson, Tom. *The Everything Kids' Science Experiments Book: Boil Ice, Float Water, Measure Gravity – Challenge the World Around You!* Avon, Massachusetts: Adams Media, 2001.

GLOSSARY

iris (EYE-ris) The round eye muscle that is colored and surrounds the pupil.

pulse (PULS) The beat of a heart.

pupil (PYOO-pul) The opening in the eye that changes size to let the right amount of light into the eye.

rays (RAYZ) Beams of light or other forms of energy.

reflection (rih-FLEK-shun) The image of something, seen on a shiny surface.

static electricity (STA-tik ih-lek-TRIH-suh-tee) A kind of electricity that can build up in objects.

Quiz Answers

Page 11 – A mirror

Page 17 – No. The pencil is made of wood.

Page 19 – A stethoscope

INDEX

WEB SITES

For Web resources related to the subject of this book, go to: www.windmillbooks.com/weblinks and select this book's title.